Lakeland
panorama

Books by W. A. Poucher
available from Constable

Scotland
Wales
The Lake District
The Highlands of Scotland
The Alps
The Yorkshire Dales
  and the Peak District
Lakeland fells
The West Country
Skye
Ireland
The magic of the
  Highlands
The magic of Skye
The Scottish Peaks
The Peak and Pennines
The Lakeland Peaks
The Welsh Peaks

Other books now out of print

The backbone of England
Climbing with a camera: the Lake District
Escape to the hills
A camera in the Cairngorms
Scotland through the lens
Highland holiday
The North Western Highlands
Lakeland scrapbook
Lakeland through the lens
Lakeland holiday
Lakeland journey
Over lakeland fells
Wanderings in Wales
Snowdonia through the lens
Snowdon holiday
Peak panorama
The Surrey hills
The magic of the Dolomites
West country journey
Journey into Ireland

LAKELAND
PANORAMA
W. A. Poucher

Constable London

First published in Great Britain 1989
by Constable and Company Limited
10 Orange Street London WC2H 7EG
Copyright © 1989 pictures, the Estate of W. A. Poucher
Copyright © 1989 text, John Poucher
ISBN 0 09 468950 4
Text filmset by Servis Filmsetting Ltd, Manchester
Printed and bound in Spain by
Graficas Estella, S. A.

The photographs

Ullswater from Sharrow Bay
(*frontispiece*)
13 Shap Abbey
14/15 Haweswater Dam
16/17 Haweswater
18/19 Mardale Head
20/21 Kentmere Reservoir
22/23 Martindale Church
24/25 Ill Bell range from Troutbeck
26/27 Gray Crag
28/29 Hayeswater Gill
30/31 Red Screes from Garburn Pass
32/33 Brothers Water
34/35 Ullswater
36/37 Ullswater from Sharrow Bay
38 Aira Force
40/41 Dove Crag and Hart Crag
42/43 Link Cove, Deepdale
44/45 St Sunday Crag
46/47 The approach to Helvellyn
48/49 Striding Edge
50/51 Red Tarn
52/53 Windermere from Orrest Head
54/55 Boats at rest
56/57 Windermere
58/59 The Langdale Pikes from Low Wood
60/61 Esthwaite Water
62/63 Hawkshead
64/65 Colour at Clappersgate
66/67 Rydal Water
68/69 Grasmere
70/71 Steel Fell
72/73 Thirlmere
74/75 St John's Vale
76/77 Mungrisedale
78/79 Blencathra
80/81 Latrigg
82/83 Bassenthwaite Lake
84/85 Derwentwater
86/87 Causey Pike
88/89 Castle Crag
90/91 Scawdell Fell from Rosthwaite
92/93 Mist over Kings How
94/95 Tarn at Leaves
96/97 Stockley Bridge

98/99 Honister Pass
100/101 Dale Head group
102/103 Eel Crags
104/105 Hindsgarth
106/107 Rannerdale
108/109 Whiteless Pike
110/111 Crummock Water
112/113 The approach to Haystacks
114/115 Reflection
116/117 Grasmoor
118/119 Ennerdale Water
120/121 Ennerdale
122 Fell Foot, Little Langdale
124/125 Mill Ghyll
126/127 Pavey Ark
128 Gimmer Crag
129 Harrison Stickle
130/131 Pike o'Stickle
132/133 Bowfell from Three Tarns
134/135 Pike o'Blisco
136/137 Yewdale Tarn
138/139 Tarn Hows
140/141 Wetherlam from Fell Gate
142/143 Great Carrs from Wetside Edge
144/145 Grey Friar from Dunnerdale
146/147 Brim Fell and Dow Crag
148/149 Coniston Water
150/151 Boo Tarn
152/153 Brown Pike from Cove Beck
154/155 Blind Tarn
156 Dow Crag
157 Coniston Old Man
158/159 Levers Water
160/161 Cockley Beck
162/163 Dunnerdale
164 The River Duddon
165 Eskdale packhorse bridge
166/167 The Ravenglass and Eskdale Railway
168/169 Harter Fell from Cockley Beck
170 St Bees Head
171 Sty Head track
172/173 Great Gable from Thornythwaite Fell
174 The Napes Ridges
176/177 The Gables from the Corridor Route
178 Lingmell and Piers Ghyll
180/181 Great End from the Corridor Route
182/183 Esk Pike and Bowfell from Great End
184/185 Esk Hause and Allen Crags
186/187 Slight Side and Scafell Pike
188/189 The Scafell group from Great Carrs
190/191 The Scafells from Harter Fell
192 Scafell Pinnacle

194/195   Pillar from Fleetwith Pike
196/197   Yewbarrow
198/199   Wasdale Head Inn
200/201   The Screes
202/203   Farewell

Preface

Some three years before he died on 5 August 1988, in his ninety-seventh year, my father, W. A. Poucher, passed on to me his large collection of colour transparencies which cover most of the mountain areas of Britain as well as those of some other countries.

Since 1980 Constable has published eleven books of his colour photographs including two of this area, which is one that he dearly loved: *The Lake District* (1982) and *Lakeland fells* (1985). I thought it would be appropriate to choose a further selection of his incomparable pictures to make a third volume portraying this beautiful region – and here it is. The pictures, which were taken over a period of years on my father's regular walking trips in these hills and fells, show – with a few exceptions – how little Lakeland has changed over the decades. I have adhered to the same plan he used, starting in the east and finishing in the west of the Lake District.

Since first visiting the fells with my father when I was about eleven years old, I have spent many happy holidays with my family exploring the hills and valleys, lakes and tarns, of this delightful region. My wife and I became so attracted to it that on our retirement we moved to our present home, so that we could continue exploring it at our leisure.

John Poucher
Gate Ghyll, High Brigham,
Cockermouth, Cumbria
1989

Shap Abbey

Situated a mile west of Shap village are the picturesque ruins of this fourteenth-century abbey.

Haweswater Dam

This vast dam was completed in 1941 by
Manchester Corporation Waterworks, enabling
them to enlarge the area of the original lake to
some 974 acres.

Haweswater

Taken from below Branstree, this picture looks
north along the lonely lake.

Mardale Head
(overleaf)

This photograph, taken during a dry period, shows Haweswater at a low ebb, with much moraine evident. Harter Fell rises prominently against the sky.

Kentmere Reservoir
(overleaf pp 20/21)

Peacefully cradled in the hills, Kentmere Reservoir is seen here from Yoke, looking towards High Street and Harter Fell with Nan Bield pass in the centre.

Martindale Church

This small isolated church serves the community of Martindale and others in the area. Deer may sometimes be seen in this vicinity.

Ill Bell range from Troutbeck

Yoke is on the right of this picturesque ridge,
with Ill Bell in the centre and Froswick on the
left. The ridge continues out of the picture
towards High Street.

Gray Crag
(overleaf)

The village of Hartsop, with Gray Crag in the background, lies close to the Kirkstone Pass road. Paths from this village lead to Boardale Hause, to Hayeswater and eventually to High Street.

Hayeswater Gill

Flowing from Hayeswater reservoir, this
enchanting stream joins Pasture Beck above
Hartsop.

Red Screes
from Garburn Pass

(*overleaf*)

Known alternatively as Kilnshaw Chimney, Red
Screes dominates the west side of the upper
regions of the Kirkstone Pass. A good path to
the top starts above Ambleside.

Brothers Water

This tranquil little stretch of water is pictured
here from Dovedale, with the ridge of Hartsop
above How seen descending on the left. Place
Fell is in the background.

Ullswater
(overleaf)

On this calm and serene day, St Sunday Crag, in the distance, is perfectly reflected in the still waters of the lake.

Ullswater from Sharrow Bay
(overleaf pp 36/37)

The viewpoint for this beautiful study of clouds and water lies on the east side of the lake opposite to Watermillock.

Aira Force

This much-visited waterfall, cascading through mossy rocks, lies near the point where the road along Ullswater joins that to Dockray.

Dove Crag
and Hart Crag
(overleaf)

These two noble crags are depicted here from the ridge of Hartsop above How which divides Dovedale and Deepdale. A walk along this ridge gives excellent views into both dales.

Link Cove, Deepdale

Link Cove is a 'hanging valley' lying under
Scrubby Crag at the head of this lonely dale.

St Sunday Crag
(overleaf)

Towering over the blue surface of Ullswater, and lightly wreathed in fine cumulus cloud, this mountain makes a perfect picture on a fine summer day.

The approach to Helvellyn
(overleaf pp 46/47)

The track rises on the flank of Birkhouse Moor and leads to Striding Edge and thence to the summit. Nethermost and Dollywaggon Pikes are to the left.

Striding Edge

From the summit of Helvellyn one can view this
fine ridge in retrospect, with the gullies of St
Sunday Crag as a backdrop.

Red Tarn
(overleaf)

Cupped between Striding and Swirral Edges, this tarn can be seen (as it is here) from the path that runs from the summit of Helvellyn along Swirral Edge.

Windermere from Orrest Head

Photographers find this a perfect viewpoint for
Windermere, most popular and largest of all the
lakes.

Boats at rest

Boats are a familiar sight on this busy lake –
both private motorboats and yachts, and larger
vessels that carry passengers from one end of
Windermere to the other.

Windermere
(overleaf)

Low brooding cloud and still water give an air of mystery to the lake in this atmospheric picture.

The Langdale Pikes from Low Wood

From this point on the shore of Windermere the
Pikes are seen to particularly good effect against
the sky.

Esthwaite Water
(overleaf)

Situated to the west of Windermere beside the
B5285, this lake is a popular resort of fishermen.
The long line of the Langdale Pikes can be seen
in the far distance.

Hawkshead

In this picturesque village, the poet William Wordsworth was once a scholar at the Grammar School which was founded in the sixteenth century.

Colour at Clappersgate

Clappersgate lies beside the River Brathay and is
renowned for the brilliant display of its azaleas
and rhododendrons in spring and early summer.

Rydal Water

(overleaf)

In this charming view of a well-known and much-loved lake, the reeds make an attractive foreground.

Grasmere

Thundery clouds and brilliant sunshine make a
dramatic picture of this charming little lake.
Helm Crag frowns in the background.

Steel Fell
(overleaf)

Although only rising to a height of just over 1,800 feet, this fell dominates the view to the west of Dunmail Raise.

Thirlmere

This Manchester reservoir can best be seen from
the road along its western side, where there are
lakeside walks to be enjoyed. The view leads the
eye to Blencathra in the distance beyond the
Vale of St John.

St John's Vale

(*overleaf*)

Beside the road which threads this pleasant vale there is a stone bridge which makes a good foreground for a picture of Blencathra. (My father's *The Lake District* includes such a picture.)

Mungrisedale

This valley lies beneath the slopes of Souther Fell, an outlier of Blencathra. It is a good starting-point for walks to Carrock Fell and other hills lying to the north of Skiddaw and Blencathra.

Blencathra

(*overleaf*)

The mountain, sometimes known as Saddleback, displays to advantage its riven southern aspect from this well-chosen viewpoint.

Latrigg

This small but charming fell near to Keswick
may be traversed as part of the ascent of
Skiddaw.

Bassenthwaite Lake
(overleaf)

This, the northernmost of the district's lakes, lies under the bulk of Skiddaw to the east. The A66 runs along its western side, partly on the line of the old railway. The lake is a venue for both fishermen and dinghy sailors.

Derwentwater
(overleaf pp 84/85)

Possibly the best sited of all the lakes, Derwentwater runs south from Keswick. This picture portrays the Jaws of Borrowdale with Castle Crag in the centre, the tree and fallen branch making a perfect foreground.

Causey Pike

This mountain may be climbed as the start of a
ridge walk ending with the descent of Grisedale
Pike.

Castle Crag

A well-known feature in Borrowdale, this rocky
outcrop may be conquered with a little
scrambling.

Scawdell Fell from Rosthwaite

(overleaf)

On Ordnance Survey maps the summit is named as 'High Spy'. It may be traversed as part of a walk over Cat Bells to Dale Head. The bridge in the foreground spans the Stonethwaite Beck.

Mist over Kings How

An eminence on Grange Fell, Kings How may
be ascended direct from Borrowdale or as part
of a walk from Rosthwaite to Watendlath and
back over Grange Fell.

Tarn at Leaves

This delightfully named tarn mirrors the sky on
Rosthwaite Fell. Pike o'Stickle, one of the
Langdale Pikes, can be seen in the distance.

Stockley Bridge
(overleaf)

This landmark, well known to walkers from Seathwaite to Sty Head or Esk Hause, lies near Seathwaite, one of the wettest places in England.

Honister Pass
(overleaf pp 98/99)

The road passing from Borrowdale to Buttermere traverses this lengthy pass. Honister Crag, an outcrop of Fleetwith Pike, dominates its upper reaches.

Dale Head group

Seen here from near Bleaberry Tarn, which lies
below Red Pike, this group of hills includes
Hindsgarth and Robinson, which with Dale
Head make a fine ridge walk. The top of
Honister Pass is a convenient starting point. The
view includes Buttermere below.

Eel Crags

(overleaf)

Seen here from Dale Head, these crags lie on the Newlands side of High Spy, and offer some rock-climbing.

Hindsgarth

(overleaf pp 104/105)

From Fleetwith Pike the forbidding crags of this mountain, above Buttermere, are seen to advantage.

Rannerdale

This valley on the northern side of Buttermere
is well known for the carpet of bluebells that
covers it in the spring.

Whiteless Pike
(overleaf)

The sharp outline of this peak is quite impressive although only just over 2,000 feet in height. This photograph shows it as it is seen from Rannerdale.

Crummock Water

The viewpoint for this panoramic photograph is
High Stile: in the middle distance is Bleaberry
Tarn, cradled by the slopes of Red Pike, with
Crummock Water beyond.

The approach to Haystacks

This delectable mountain with its charming
tarns may be reached from the summit of
Honister Pass via the ruins of the Drum House.
This is one of my favourite walks. High Crag
can just be seen on the extreme right.

Reflection
(overleaf)

Only the outline of Haystacks can be seen in this striking photograph, mirrored in the placid waters of Buttermere.

Grasmoor
(overleaf pp 116/117)

Seen, as it is here, from beside Crummock Water, this mountain is at its most imposing. It may easily be climbed, via Gasgale Ghyll, from Lanthwaite Green.

Ennerdale Water
(overleaf pp 118/119)

The Anglers Inn which once stood here is, alas, no more, but from its site the lake, with Pillar and its satellites in the distance, makes a fine picture.

Ennerdale

Some time ago the Forestry Commission, whose
plantations now dominate this valley,
constructed The Nine Becks Walk which starts
from the forest road to Black Sail and traverses
under Pillar. This is where it begins.

Fell Foot, Little Langdale

This pretty, whitewashed farmhouse stands near the junction of the road from Great Langdale via Blea Tarn and that which runs along Little Langdale to Wrynose Pass.

Mill Ghyll

(overleaf)

A path alongside this ghyll in Langdale, with its tumbling waterfalls, starts near the New Dungeon Ghyll Hotel, and climbs to Stickle Tarn under Pavey Ark.

Pavey Ark

Seen here from the path to Harrison Stickle,
with Stickle Tarn below it, Pavey Ark is one of
the imposing Langdale Pikes.

Gimmer Crag

(overleaf)

This fine crag in the Langdale Pikes has for
years been among the most favoured
playgrounds of Lake District rock-climbers. It
lies not far from the Old Dungeon Ghyll Hotel.

Harrison Stickle

(overleaf p 129)

With a height of 2,403 feet, this is the highest of
the Langdale Pikes. It is seen here from the path
up the Band which leads to Bowfell.

Pike o' Stickle

Taken from near Rosset Ghyll, this picture
shows to perfection the characteristic outline of
Pike o'Stickle.

Bowfell
from Three Tarns

(overleaf)

Three Tarns lie between Bowfell and Crinkle
Crags, and they make a fine foreground for this
picture which displays Bowfell to such good
effect.

Pike o' Blisco

The viewpoint here is Mickle Door on Crinkle
Crags, and it shows off the fine shape of the
mountain, which may be ascended from Great
Langdale or from the top of Wrynose Pass via
Red Tarn.

Yewdale Tarn

This beautiful little tarn lies beside the road
from Ambleside to Coniston, and anglers may
often be seen here.

Tarn Hows
(overleaf)

This justly renowned beauty spot is not far from Coniston, and in the summer it attracts crowds of visitors. Here, though, it is captured superbly on a quiet autumn day.

Wetherlam from Fell Gate
(overleaf pp 140/141)

One of the Coniston group, Wetherlam is seen here from Fell Gate which marks the end of the steep road out of the village. One pleasant way to the top starts at Tilberthwaite.

Great Carrs from Wetside Edge

Wetside Edge lies between the Greenburn valley
and Wrynose Pass. If you are descending from it
to the head of the pass, the cairn that can be
seen in the picture is the key to where the path
turns off.

Grey Friar from Dunnerdale

Probably the least visited of the Coniston fells,
this mountain is a good viewpoint for the
Scafells.

Brim Fell
and Dow Crag
(overleaf)

Once you have climbed one of the Coniston
fells, the ridge walking here is easy and pleasant.
The track passes over Brim Fell. Dow Crag,
with Goats Water below, is a preserve of the
rock-climber.

Coniston Water

Low-lying mist over the silvery lake lends a
romantic and dreamy beauty to this scene.

Boo Tarn

Now more overgrown than when this picture
was taken, Boo Tarn lies beside the Walna Scar
'road', not far from Fell Gate. The 'road' is used
by walkers from Coniston to Dunnerdale.

Brown Pike from Cove Beck

The Walna Scar 'road' passes over Cove Beck
by this bridge. Brown Pike is the southern end
of the ridge that includes Buck Pike and Dow
Crag.

Blind Tarn
(overleaf)

Cradled between the slopes of Brown and Buck Pikes, this deserted little pool is so called because it has no discernible outlet. Beyond it stretches a fine panorama.

Dow Crag
(overleaf p 156)

The cairn in the foreground is to be found on the track from the Walna Scar 'road' to Goats Water, which lies beneath the jutting buttresses of Dow Crag.

Coniston Old Man
(overleaf p 157)

Taken from Dow Crag, this picture reveals the Old Man in the distance, with Goats Water below. The Old Man was once a mountain of Lancashire, but since the redefinition of county boundaries, it now lies within Cumbria.

Levers Water

Below Brim Fell lies this shining tarn, whose
outlet, Levers Water Beck, joins Red Dell Beck
to form Church Beck, which flows down
through Coniston to the lake.

Cockley Beck
(overleaf)

Cockley Beck lies near the junction of the road to Wrynose Pass from Eskdale via Hardknott Pass, and the road along Dunnerdale. The signpost tells all.

Dunnerdale
(overleaf pp 162/163)

Known to some as the Duddon Valley, Dunnerdale in its autumn colours is enchanting – as can be seen in the brilliant tapestry captured here.

The River Duddon
(overleaf p 164)

It is a delight to while away a summer's day on the banks of the River Duddon, as it flows down Dunnerdale through many miniature falls and gorges.

Eskdale packhorse bridge
(overleaf p 165)

This is a particularly fine example of a pleasing old-style construction. Many others are to be found in the district.

The Ravenglass and Eskdale Railway

The narrow-gauge railway that in summer
carries trains between Ravenglass and Dalegarth
in Eskdale was first opened for goods traffic in
1875, and to passengers in 1876. It is now an
attraction for holiday-makers, and is sometimes
referred to as 'La'al Ratty'.

Harter Fell
from Cockley Beck
(*overleaf*)

Harter Fell lies between Eskdale and Dunnerdale and may be ascended from either valley – but my own choice of route starts in Eskdale.

St Bees Head
(*overleaf p 170*)

The sheer sandstone cliffs of this promontory, soaring above the waves, are the haunt of numerous screeching sea-birds.

Sty Head track
(*overleaf p 171*)

Running from Seathwaite in Borrowdale to Wasdale, over Sty Head Pass, this track is much used by walkers heading for Great Gable or the Scafells.

Great Gable from Thornythwaite Fell

The viewpoint on Thornythwaite Fell of this
imposing peak is passed during the ascent of
Glaramara from Borrowdale.

The Napes Ridges

Lying on the southern flank of Great Gable, these ridges offer numerous climbs for the enthusiast. Napes Needle is clearly seen in this picture, which is taken from the Climbers Traverse.

The Gables from the Corridor Route
(*overleaf*)

The Corridor, or Guides, Route runs from Sty Head Pass to the Lingmell Col and eventually leads to Scafell Pike. On Great Gable itself, both Great Hell Gate scree and the Breast Route track leading to the summit of the mountain are clearly visible.

Lingmell and Piers Ghyll

Piers Ghyll is a vast cleft which contains many rock-climbing pitches, and its exploration should be left to the expert climber.

Great End from the Corridor Route

(overleaf)

The Corridor Route passes the entrance to Skew Ghyll which offers a good scramble to the summit of Great End for those competent in this sport.

Esk Pike and Bowfell from Great End

Esk Pike lies above the track from Langdale to
Esk Hause, and is separated from Bowfell by
Ore Gap. This picture shows the frowning face
that Esk Pike presents to Eskdale.

Esk Hause and Allen Crags

Allen Crags lie at the southern end of the ridge
running from Borrowdale over Glaramara. The
traverse of these rough fells makes a delightful
walk.

Slight Side
and Scafell Pike
(overleaf)

The grassy slope of Slight Side, which is an outlier of Scafell and is seen here from the Taw House track above Eskdale, dominates the foreground. Scafell Pike is on the right.

The Scafell group
from Great Carrs
(overleaf pp 188/189)

Great Carrs in the Coniston fells provides an excellent viewpoint for the central fells which are dominated by the bulk of the Scafells.

The Scafells
from Harter Fell
(overleaf pp 190/191)

From Harter Fell, Upper Eskdale leads the eye to the magnificent Scafell group.

Scafell Pinnacle

The steep crags of Scafell are the joy of the
rock-climber, and offer many routes of varying
severity.

Pillar from Fleetwith Pike

From here, Pillar Fell is viewed over Haystacks.
It may be climbed from Wasdale or Ennerdale.
Pillar Rock lies on the Ennerdale side below the
summit.

Yewbarrow
(*overleaf*)

This shapely mountain rises near the head of
Wastwater and is seen here from the narrow
road which traverses Wasdale.

Wasdale Head Inn

Beloved of generations of climbers, this inn
offers sustenance to all who visit Wasdale Head.

The Screes

(overleaf)

Falling to Wastwater from Illgill Head, The Screes, captured here in the low evening light, reveal a marvellous array of colours.

Farewell

(overleaf pp 202/203)

With its glorious autumn colouring and superb evening cloudscape, this view of the hills surrounding Wasdale is a fitting end to our journey through this beautiful region.